"The sea, once it casts its spell, holds one in its net of wonder forever."

- Jacques Cousteau

"The ocean is a mighty harmonist."

- William Wordsworth

"The ocean is a reminder of the cycle of birth, death, and rebirth, and the impermanence of all things."

- Buddha

"The sea is a symbol of freedom, of adventure, and of the unknown."

- Nikolai Gogol

"The ocean is a symbol of the power of the divine, and its vastness fills us with wonder and awe."

- Ramakrishna Paramahamsa

"We know only too well that what we are doing is nothing more than a drop in the ocean. But if the drop were not there, the ocean would be missing something."

- Mother Teresa

"The sea is only the embodiment of a supernatural and wonderful existence. It is nothing but love and emotion; it is the Living Infinite." ,

- Jules Verne

"The ocean stirs the
heart, inspires the
imagination, and
brings eternal joy to
the soul."

- Wyland

"The sea is a desert of waves, a wilderness of water."

- Langston Hughes

Sea Grapes

"That sail which leans
on light,
tired of islands,
a schooner beating up
the Caribbean

for home, could be
Odysseus,
home-bound on the
Aegean;
that father and
husband's

longing, under gnarled
sour grapes, is
like the adulterer
hearing Nausicaa's
name
in every gull's outcry.

This brings nobody
peace. The ancient war
between obsession and
responsibility

will never finish and has
been the same

for the sea-wanderer or
the one on shore
now wriggling on his
sandals to walk home,
since Troy sighed its last
flame,

and the blind giant's
boulder heaved the
trough
from whose
groundswell the great
hexameters come
to the conclusions of
exhausted surf.

The classics can
console. But not
enough."

- Derek Walcott

"The sea is the same as it has been since before men ever went on it in boats."

- Ernest Hemingway

"The sea, the great unifier, is man's only hope. Now, as never before, the old phrase has a literal meaning: we are all in the same boat."

- Jacques Yves Cousteau

"In the depths of the sea, you can't see beyond a few meters, but you can sense the presence of an unknown realm."

- Ryuichi Sakamoto

"The ocean is a reminder of the interconnectedness of all things, and our responsibility to protect the earth and its creatures."

- Jane Goodall

"The sea is not a gift bestowed by Nature but a common property that should be available to all men, like the air."

- Roman Rolland

The Sea and the Skylark

"On ear and ear two noises too old to
end
Trench—right, the tide that ramps
against the shore;
With a flood or a fall, low lull-off or
all roar,
Frequenting there while moon shall
wear and wend.
Left hand, off land, I hear the lark
ascend,
His rash-fresh re-winded new-skeinèd
score
In crisps of curl off wild winch whirl,
and pour
And pelt music, till none's to spill nor
spend.

(...)

(...)

How these two shame this shallow and
frail town!
How ring right out our sordid turbid
time,
Being pure! We, life's pride and cared-
for crown,
Have lost that cheer and charm of
earth's past prime:
Our make and making break, are
breaking, down
To man's last dust, drain fast towards
man's first slime.

- Gerard Manley Hopkins

"The ocean is a central image. It is the symbolism of a great journey."

- Enya

"The breaking of a wave cannot explain the whole sea."

- Vladimir Nabokov

"Towards thee I roll, thou all-destroying but unconquering whale; to the last I grapple with thee; from hell's heart I stab at thee; for hate's sake I spit my last breath at thee."

- Herman Melville

"The ocean is a source of inspiration for artists, writers, and scientists alike. It has the power to transport us to another world."

- Mikhail Lermontov

"The ocean is a symbol of the eternal, and its depths contain secrets that are yet to be discovered."

- Osho

"The ocean is a mighty force, and it is up to us to respect and protect it."

- Sylvia Earle

Sea Shell

"Sea Shell, Sea Shell,
Sing me a song, O Please!
A song of ships, and sailor men,
And parrots, and tropical trees,

Of islands lost in the Spanish Main
Which no man ever may find again,
Of fishes and corals under the waves,
And seahorses stabled in great green
caves.

Sea Shell, Sea Shell,
Sing of the things you know so well."

-Amy Lowell

"The ocean is a beautiful, magnificent creature that demands respect."

- Clint Eastwood

"The sea, the great unifier, is man's only hope. Now, as never before, the old phrase has a literal meaning: we are all in the same boat."

- Jacques Yves Cousteau

"The ocean is a reminder of the need for balance and harmony in our lives, and the importance of respecting nature."

- Dalai Lama

"The sea is a symbol of the cycle of life, of birth, death, and rebirth."

- Yevgeny Yevtushenko

"The sea is a desert of waves, a
wilderness of water."

- Langston Hughes

The Sea Poem

"The sea is a hungry dog,
Giant and grey.
He rolls on the beach all day.
With his clashing teeth and shaggy jaws
Hour upon hour he gnaws
The rumbling, tumbling stones,
And 'Bones, bones, bones, bones! '
The giant sea-dog moans,
Licking his greasy paws.
And when the night wind roars
And the moon rocks in the stormy cloud,
He bounds to his feet and snuffs and sniffs,
Shaking his wet sides over the cliffs,
And howls and hollos long and loud.
But on quiet days in May or June,
When even the grasses on the dune
Play no more their reedy tune,
With his head between his paws
He lies on the sandy shores,

So quiet, so quiet, he scarcely snores."

- James Reeves

"The ocean is a symbol of the power of the human spirit, and its waves represent the challenges we face and overcome in life."

- Swami Vivekananda

"The ocean is the lifeblood of our world. If we were to lose our fish that we appreciate so much by overfishing; or if we were to lose some of our favorite beaches to overbuilding and pollution, then how would we feel? It's become a case of not knowing what you've got until it's gone."

- Aaron Peirsol

"The sea is a reminder of the power of nature, and of our own small place in the world."

- Anton Chekhov

"Waves are the voices of tides. Tides are life."

- Tamora Pierce

"The ocean is a place of paradox, where life exists in abundance despite the scarcity of essential resources."

- Werner Herzog

"The ocean is a reminder of the power of nature, and of our own small place in the world."

- Alexander Solzhenitsyn

"The sea, with its endless horizon, is one of the most beautiful and inspiring sights in the world."

- Jeff Rann

Sea-Fever

"I must go down to the seas again, to the lonely sea and the sky,
And all I ask is a tall ship and a star to steer her by;
And the wheel's kick and the wind's song and the white sail's shaking,
And a grey mist on the sea's face, and a grey dawn breaking.

I must go down to the seas again, for the call of the running tide
Is a wild call and a clear call that may not be denied;

And all I ask is a windy day with the white clouds flying,
And the flung spray and the blown spume, and the sea-gulls crying.

I must go down to the seas again, to the vagrant gypsy life,
To the gull's way and the whale's way where the wind's like a whetted knife;
And all I ask is a merry yarn from a laughing fellow-rover,
And quiet sleep and a sweet dream when the long trick's over."

- John Masefielf

"The sea is a vast, mysterious place
that can inspire feelings of awe,
wonder, and even fear."

- Brian Skerry

"I love the sea's sounds and the way it reflects the sky. The colours that shimmer across its surface are unbelievable."

- John Dyer

"The ocean is a vast and wondrous place, full of life, mystery, and wonder."

- Ivan Turgenev

"The ocean is a world of its own, full of incredible beauty and mystery."

- David Attenborough

"The ocean is a mystery that has always fascinated me. It is a place of wonder, a place where anything can happen."

- Sergey Brin

"The sea is everything. It covers seven tenths of the terrestrial globe. Its breath is pure and healthy. It is an immense desert, where man is never lonely, for he feels life stirring on all sides."

- Jules Verne

"The sea is a source of wonder and inspiration for people of all ages and backgrounds."

- David Doubilet

"The ocean is a living, breathing entity that deserves our respect and protection."

- Sylvia Earle

"The ocean is a place of wonder and awe, a place that never ceases to amaze and inspire."

- Andrey Tarkovsky

"The sea complains upon a thousand shores."

- Alexander Smith

The Ocean

"The Ocean has its silent caves,
Deep, quiet, and alone;
Though there be fury on the waves,
Beneath them there is none.

The awful spirits of the deep
Hold their communion there;
And there are those for whom we
weep,
The young, the bright, the fair.

Calmly the wearied seamen rest
Beneath their own blue sea.
The ocean solitudes are blest,
For there is purity.

The earth has guilt, the earth has care,
Unquiet are its graves;
But peaceful sleep is ever there,
Beneath the dark blue waves."

- Nathaniel Hawthorne

"The sea is a place of transformation, a place where we can leave our troubles behind and become something new."

- Anna Akhmatova

"The ocean is a magnificent canvas that ignites my imagination and passion."

- Wayde van Niekerk

"The sea is a symbol of hope, of renewal, and of the endless possibilities of the future."

- Daniil Kharms

Dover Beach

"The sea is calm tonight.
The tide is full, the moon lies fair
Upon the straits; on the French coast the light
Gleams and is gone; the cliffs of England stand,
Glimmering and vast, out in the tranquil bay.
Come to the window, sweet is the night-air!
Only, from the long line of spray
Where the sea meets the moon-blanched land,
Listen! you hear the grating roar
Of pebbles which the waves draw back, and fling,
At their return, up the high strand,
Begin, and cease, and then again begin,
With tremulous cadence slow, and bring
The eternal note of sadness in.

Sophocles long ago
Heard it on the Ægean, and it brought
Into his mind the turbid ebb and flow
Of human misery; we
Find also in the sound a thought,
Hearing it by this distant northern sea.

(...)

(...)

The Sea of Faith
Was once, too, at the full, and round earth's shore
Lay like the folds of a bright girdle furled.
But now I only hearIts melancholy, long,
withdrawing roar,
Retreating, to the breath
Of the night-wind, down the vast edges drear
And naked shingles of the world.

Ah, love, let us be true
To one another! for the world, which seems
To lie before us like a land of dreams,
So various, so beautiful, so new,
Hath really neither joy, nor love, nor light,
Nor certitude, nor peace, nor help for pain;
And we are here as on a darkling plain
Swept with confused alarms of struggle and flight,
Where ignorant armies clash by night."

- Matthew Arnold

"The ocean is a mighty force that moves the world."

- Ernest Agyemang Yeboah

"The sea is a great teacher, showing us the beauty of life, the power of nature, and the importance of community."

- Jacques Yves Cousteau

"The waves of the
sea help me get back
to me."

- Jill Davis

"The ocean has always been a salve to
my soul."

- Jimmy Buffett

"The ocean is a mighty harmonist."

- William Wordsworth

"The sea is a place of mystery, of adventure, and of endless possibility."

- Vladimir Mayakovsky

"The ocean is a source of life, a place where all living creatures come together in a delicate balance."

- Boris Pasternak

"The ocean is a beautiful place to live and surf, but it can be a dangerous place if you don't respect it."

- Bethany Hamilton

"The ocean is the cradle of life, the source of inspiration, and the essence of beauty."

- APJ Abdul Kalam

"The voice of the sea speaks
to the soul."

- Kate Chopin

"The ocean is a symbol
of the human spirit, of
our innate desire to
explore and to discover
the unknown."

- Mikhail Bulgakov

"The ocean is a symbol of power, strength, life, mystery, hope, and truth."

- Debasish Mridha

By The Sea

"I started early, took my dog,
And visited the sea;
The mermaids in the basement
Came out to look at me.

And frigates in the upper floor
Extended hempen hands,
Presuming me to be a mouse
Aground, upon the sands.

But no man moved me till the tide
Went past my simple shoe,
And past my apron and my belt,
And past my bodice too,

(...)

(...)

And made as he would eat me up
As wholly as a dew
Upon a dandelion's sleeve —
And then I started too.

And he — he followed close behind;
I felt his silver heel
Upon my ankle, — then my shoes
Would overflow with pearl.

Until we met the solid town,
No man he seemed to know;
And bowing with a mighty look
At me, the sea withdrew."

- Emily Dickinson

"The ocean is a reminder of the impermanence of life, and the need to cherish every moment."

- Rumi

"The sea, once it casts its spell, holds one in its net of wonder forever."

- Jacques Yves Cousteau

"The ocean is a symbol of the interconnectedness of all life, and our responsibility to protect it."

- Vandana Shiva

"The sea is nothing but a library of all the tears in history."

- Lemony Snicket

"The ocean is a source of peace and tranquility, and its rhythms soothe our souls."

- Sri Sri Ravi Shankar

"The ocean is a great teacher. It teaches us that all things are interconnected and that we must respect and protect its fragile ecosystem."

- Mikhail Gorbachev

"Waves are not measured in feet or inches, they are measured in increments of fear."

- Buzzy Trent

"The ocean is a symbol of the mystery of existence, and our place in the universe."

- Deepak Chopra

"The ocean is a wilderness reaching round the globe, wilder than a Bengal jungle, and fuller of monsters, washing the very wharves of our cities and the gardens of our sea-side residences."

- Henry David Thoreau

"The ocean is a vast reservoir of nature's beauty and wonder."

- Rabindranath Tagore

"The ocean is a symbol of the power of the feminine, and its waves represent the ebb and flow of life."

- Amma

"The ocean is a place of skin, rich outer membranes hiding thick juicy insides, laden with the soup of being."

- Vassar Miller

"The sea is like music. It has all the dreams of the soul within itself and sounds them out."

- Alexander Pushkin

"The sea is a symbol of eternity, of vastness, of life itself."

- Lev Tolstoy

"The sea is a dangerous place, but
it's also a place of freedom and joy.
It's a place where you can forget
your worries and just let go."

- Sara Bareilles

"The ocean is a reminder of the vastness of creation, and the insignificance of our individual selves."

- Jiddu Krishnamurti

"The sea does not reward those who are too anxious, too greedy, or too impatient. To dig for treasures shows not only impatience and greed, but lack of faith. Patience, patience, patience, is what the sea teaches. Patience and faith."

- Anne Morrow Lindbergh

"The ocean is a symbol of the richness of life, and the abundance of nature's blessings."

- Sadhguru

"The ocean is a reflection of our inner selves, deep and mysterious."

- Mahatma Gandhi

The Shark

"He seemed to know
the harbour,
So leisurely he swam;
His fin,
Like a piece of sheet-
iron,
Three-cornered,
And with knife-edge,
Stirred not a bubble
As it moved
With its base-line on
the water.

His body was tubular
And tapered
And smoke-blue,
And as he passed the
wharf
He turned,
And snapped at a flat-
fish
That was dead and
floating.

And I saw the flash of
a white throat,
And a double row of
white teeth,
And eyes of metallic
grey,
Hard and narrow and
slit.

Then out of the
harbour,
With that three-
cornered fin
Shearing without a
bubble the water
Lithely,
Leisurely,
He swam—
That strange fish,
Tubular, tapered,
smoke-blue,
Part vulture, part wolf,
Part neither—for his
blood was cold."

- Edwin John Pratt

"The sea, once it casts its spell, holds one in its net of wonder forever."

- Jacques Yves Cousteau

"The sea is a reflection of infinite beauty and power."

- Fyodor Dostoevsky

"The ocean is the source of all life, and its protection is our duty."

- Narendra Modi

"The sea is a mirror of the soul, reflecting our hopes, dreams, and fears."

- Marina Tsvetaeva

"The ocean is a source of inspiration for artists, poets, and mystics, who seek to capture its beauty and mystery."

- Kabir

"The ocean is a symbol of resilience, of strength, and of endurance."

- Maxim Gorky

"The ocean is a symbol of the power of nature, and its majesty fills us with awe."

- Jawaharlal Nehru

The Fish

"I caught a tremendous fish
and held him beside the boat
half out of water, with my hook
fast in a corner of his mouth.
He didn't fight.
He hadn't fought at all.
He hung a grunting weight,
battered and venerable
and homely. Here and there
his brown skin hung in strips
like ancient wallpaper,
and its pattern of darker brown
was like wallpaper:
shapes like full-blown roses
stained and lost through age.
He was speckled with barnacles,
fine rosettes of lime,
and infested
with tiny white sea-lice,
and underneath two or three
rags of green weed hung down.

(...)

(...)

While his gills were breathing in
the terrible oxygen
—the frightening gills,
fresh and crisp with blood,
that can cut so badly—
I thought of the coarse white flesh
packed in like feathers,
the big bones and the little bones,
the dramatic reds and blacks
of his shiny entrails,
and the pink swim-bladder
like a big peony.
I looked into his eyes
which were far larger than mine
but shallower, and yellowed,
the irises backed and packed
with tarnished tinfoil
seen through the lenses
of old scratched isinglass.
They shifted a little, but not
to return my stare.
—It was more like the tipping
of an object toward the light.

(...)

(...)

I admired his sullen face,
the mechanism of his jaw,
and then I saw
that from his lower lip
—if you could call it a lip—
grim, wet, and weaponlike,
hung five old pieces of fish-line,
or four and a wire leader
with the swivel still attached,
with all their five big hooks
grown firmly in his mouth.
A green line, frayed at the end
where he broke it, two heavier lines,
and a fine black thread
still crimped from the strain and snap
when it broke and he got away.
Like medals with their ribbons
frayed and wavering,
a five-haired beard of wisdom
trailing from his aching jaw.

(...)

(...)

stared and stared
and victory filled up
the little rented boat,
from the pool of bilge
where oil had spread a rainbow
around the rusted engine
to the bailer rusted orange,
the sun-cracked thwarts,
the oarlocks on their strings,
the gunnels—until everything
was rainbow, rainbow, rainbow!
And I let the fish go.

- Elizabeth Bishop

"The ocean is a symbol of the divine, vast and infinite."

- Sri Aurobindo

Printed in Great Britain
by Amazon

37096437R00056